WILD MOON

How the Lunar Phases Light Up Our World

Andie Powers   art by Lucy Rose

Gibbs Smith

I AM THE MOON.

Your moon. Their moon.

Wild moon.

The moon's **orbit** around the earth is about 27 days.

We only see one side of the moon because it rotates at the same speed that it revolves around the earth. This is called **synchronous rotation**.

When it is day on one side of the earth, it is night on the other.

While you sleep, I am moving. I am spinning.
I dance in an oval around the earth. Pirouette! Pirouette!
I hum a lullaby to this side of the planet and then to the other.

While you dream, I am rising.
Up over the horizon, I peek from behind the earth's shadow.
I catch the sun's rays on my face in eight different ways.
Each phase is the same from ocean to ocean.

Moonrise *is the time of day when the moon rises above the earth's horizon.*

The sun's rays reflecting off the moon's surface creates the effect of moonlight.

While you grow, I am pulling. I am tugging.
The oceans reach for me. They form tides.
The limpet clings to rock. The shorebird feeds.

*The moon's **tidal force** (or gravitational pull) causes oceans to bulge toward it, making high tides.*

NEW MOON

When I am a new moon, I am gazing—
out at the stars that twinkle in the peaceful darkness.
The earth is still and slumbering.

My new moon is for hiding.
Prey, stay close, stay cautious, stay warm in your dens.

Prey animals like antelopes and zebras cannot see well during the dark new moon. They must stay close to their herd to avoid predators.

My new moon is for hunting. Predator, follow your night's eye and bring food to the cubs.

Lions use their natural night vision to hunt during the darkest phases of the moon.

WAXING CRESCENT

When I am a waxing crescent, I am smiling, star to star.
First, a sliver of light, then a grin!
I am a door slowly creaking open.

When moonlight is low, the dung beetle uses the bright stars of the Milky Way to navigate home.

My waxing crescent is for scurrying.
Scamper-scurry, turn, stop, see!
My low glow helps the Milky Way to shine and guide you home.

White barn owls use their bright white feathers to stun prey in the moonlight.

FIRST QUARTER

When I am a first quarter, I am winking.
You can see one quarter of me, because I am as round as a bubble.
I float in space and will never turn my back to you.
I hide in nooks and crannies, hills and valleys.

Small animals like the wood mouse avoid brighter phases of the moon, because they are more likely to be seen by predators.

My first quarter is for waking, foraging, and finding. Stretch your sleepy limbs and blink your bright eyes. Time to wake and work!

It is for sneaking and searching. Use my light to see what might be lurking. Find seeds and scamper safely away.

WAXING GIBBOUS

When I am a waxing gibbous, I am stretching. I am alive!
I wash the land with light. My reflection on the lake is shining.
I am ready to fold out my edges and crow. Here I go!

My waxing gibbous is for glowing.
Glow, little beauty, blue in my light.
Show enemies your battle colors.
Creep quietly into crevices.

Many species of scorpion glow-in-the-dark under bright moonlight, which may help them find dark places to hide or help them see other scorpions. This is called **biofluorescence**.

FULL MOON

When I am a full moon, I am beaming BRIGHT! My light is so bright that birds sing before dawn.

The bright light of a full moon causes white-browed sparrow weavers to sing and hunt insects before dawn.

My full moon is for howling.
Howl together in the moonlit night to protect your pack.
Hunt with ears alert and eyes aglow.

Gray wolves are active at night. They don't howl at the moon, but they do howl to communicate with their pack and to warn rivals to stay away. They have special reflectors in their eyes to help them see in the dark. These reflectors make their eyes appear to glow in the moonlight.

My full moon is for nesting. Return to the island of your birth to find your mate, to nest, and to hatch your eggs.

Barau's petrels return to Réunion Island, near Madagascar, each year to mate and nest during a full moon.

My full moon is for spawning.
When light and time and warmth collide, a snowstorm of eggs bursts toward the water's surface. A swirling flurry of life that is visible all the way up here in space.

*Coral in the Great Barrier Reef releases its **gametes** (eggs and sperm) into the ocean for breeding. There are so many that the mass spawn is visible from space.*

Supermoon

Micromoon

Sometimes my full moon is special. When I spin close to the earth on my oval loop, I seem to grow, like a balloon filling up with air.

When I spin farther away, I shrink small like a speck, a sparkle.

Blood Moon

And when the sun and I play hide-and-seek, and she dips down behind the earth, I am painted red.

Watch me eclipse

A lunar eclipse occurs when the sun, the earth, and the moon align, causing the sun's rays to bend around the earth. The atmosphere absorbs every color except red, which shines on the moon.

WANING GIBBOUS

When I am a waning gibbous, I am dipping—
my toes into darkness. Edges blurring.
I'm beginning to melt like a scoop of ice cream.

Sand hoppers use moonlight to navigate between the sand and shore.

My waning gibbous is for hopping.
Hop, hop. Munch, munch.
Use the low tide to gather food.
Use my light to keep the sea in view.

LAST QUARTER

When I am a last quarter, I am retreating.
Not quite gone, beginning to yawn.
Sunset on my hills. Sunset on my valleys.

My last quarter is for creaking.
Creeeaaakk. Open your shell to calm currents
and wait for plankton, then slurp them up!

Oysters open and close their shells according to the moon phases. They are closed more during fuller moon phases and begin to open with less light.

Earthshine occurs when the sunlight reflecting off the earth casts a dim glow on the hidden side of the moon, making it faintly visible.

WANING CRESCENT

When I am a waning crescent, I am closing. Winking, blinking, nodding off. I might bask in your earthshine. A ghost moon.

My waning crescent is for flying.
Raise your wings, spread your tail, and set off south with the last sliver of my light.

When it is time to migrate to warmer temperatures in the fall, European nightjars fill their bellies with insects during well-lit nights. Then, they time their migration departures for nights with less moonlight. This is usually about ten days after the full moon.

My waning crescent is for preparing. Drink, graze, and seek out safety before darkness returns.

My waning crescent is for pacing.
Wait for the shadows and plan the hunt to fill your hungry bellies.
Fly, snatch, run, and catch.

And all this while you are sleeping,
you are dreaming,
you are growing.

I am here, always moving,
always rising,
always spinning.

Your moon. Their moon.
Wild moon.

MOON PHASES

The way the moon appears to the earth during different stages of its orbit is called a "moon phase." The moon has eight phases. The lunar cycle lasts approximately 29.5 days.

NEW MOON: The moon looks invisible! When the moon sits between the earth and the sun, its face is not illuminated for us to see. It is also up during the day!

WAXING CRESCENT: Waxing means to grow, and a crescent is the shape of a curve or smile. As the nights go on, more light from the sun reflects off the moon, so it looks like a growing crescent. It begins to rise later and later.

FIRST QUARTER: The moon has finished one fourth of its orbit around the earth. To us, it looks like one half of a circle. In its first quarter, the moon rises at noon and sets at midnight.

WAXING GIBBOUS: The moon is in this phase when we can see almost a whole, illuminated circle. It is in its waxing gibbous phase until it is 99.9 percent full.

FULL MOON: A full moon phase means the moon has finished half of its orbit around the earth! The moon is fully illuminated, meaning we can see a full circle. The full moon rises at sunset and sets at dawn.

WANING GIBBOUS: Waning means decreasing. During a waning gibbous phase, the illuminated side of the moon begins to shrink in the opposite direction. It rises later and later each night.

LAST QUARTER: This phase can also be called a third quarter. The moon has completed three quarters of its orbit. The moon rises at midnight and sets at noon—the opposite of a first quarter.

WANING CRESCENT: The moon is nearly finished with its orbit around the earth and appears smaller. From the earth, we can see a thinning sliver of moon as it gradually takes its place between us and the sun.

TRADITIONAL FULL MOON NAMES

The sources of the names of each month's full moon are not clear. Some historians credit many Native American tribes for versions of the names, which were then adopted and popularized by early Colonial Americans.

JANUARY
Wolf moon

FEBRUARY
Snow moon

JULY
Buck moon

AUGUST
Sturgeon moon

MARCH
Worm moon

APRIL
Pink moon

SEPTEMBER
Harvest moon

OCTOBER
Hunter's moon

MAY
Flower moon

JUNE
Strawberry moon

NOVEMBER
Beaver moon

DECEMBER
Cold moon

WHAT IS A BLUE MOON?

The moon completes twelve lunar cycles around the earth each year, but there are about eleven more days on the calendar. This means that every couple of years, we will see thirteen full moons in twelve months. When this happens, one lucky month gets two full moons! A second full moon in one calendar month is called a **blue moon**.

To the man who lassoed the Moon.
—A.P.

To Gill, for always being there.
—L.R.

First Edition
29 28 27 26 25   5 4 3 2 1

Text © 2025 Andie Powers
Illustrations © 2025 Lucy Rose

All rights reserved. No part of this book may be reproduced by any means whatsoever without written permission from the publisher, except brief portions quoted for purpose of review. No part of this book may be used or reproduced in any manner for the purpose of training artificial intelligence technologies or systems.

Published by
Gibbs Smith
570 N. Sportsplex Dr.
Kaysville, Utah 84037

1.800.835.4993 orders
www.gibbs-smith.com

Designed by Ryan Thomann
Manufactured in Guangdong, China in June 2025 by RRD Asia Printing Solutions

This product is made of FSC®-certified and other controlled material.

Library of Congress Control Number: 2024951477
ISBN: 978-1-4236-6744-5